THE MOST REQUESTED
Acoustic Songs

Cherry Lane Music Company
Director of Publications/Project Editor: Mark Phillips

ISBN 978-1-4584-0306-3

Visit our website at www.cherrylaneprint.com

CONTENTS

About a Girl

Words and Music by
Kurt Cobain

fit this shoe, __ I do, but you have a ___ clue.
num - ber to, ___ I do, keep a date with __ you.

I'll take ad - van - tage while __ you hang me

To Coda out to dry, __ but I can't see you ev - 'ry night __

free. I do.

CODA

I can't see you ev-'ry night __

free. _____ I do.

I do. _____ I

do. _____ I do.

American Pie

Words and Music by
Don McLean

may - be they'd be hap - py _____ for a while.

But Feb - ru - ar - y made me shiv - er with ev - 'ry pa - per I'd de - liv - er.

Bad news on the door - step, I could - n't take one more step. I

can't re - mem - ber if I cried when I read a - bout ___ his wid owed bride.

This - 'll be the day ___ that I ___ die. ___

1. Did you ___ write the book of love ___ and do you ___
2.-4. *(See additional lyrics)*

___ have faith in God a - bove? ___ If the Bi - ble tells ___

___ you so. ___ Now do you ___ be - lieve ___ in

11

Man, I dig those rhy-thm and blues. _____ I was a lone-ly teen-age _____ bronc-in' buck _ with a pink car-na - tion and a pick - up truck. _ But I knew I ____ was out _____ of luck _ the day _ the mu - sic died. ___

1 - 3 | 4

D7   D7   G   C

I start-ed sing-ing   He was sing-in' bye - bye Miss A-

G   D   G   C   G   D

mer - i - can Pie___ drove my Chev-y to the lev-ee but the lev-ee was dry.___ Them

G   C   G   D

good ole boys___ were drink-in' whis-key and rye,___ sing-in'

Em   A7

this - 'll be the day___ that I___ die.

man there said the mu-sic would-n't play.___ And in the streets the chil-dren screamed,_ the lov-ers cried_ and the po-ets dreamed._ But not a word was spo-ken, the church bells all were bro-ken. And the three men I ad-mire most, the Fa-ther, Son and the Ho-ly Ghost, they caught the last train for the coast the

Additional Lyrics

2. Now for ten years we've been on our own,
   And moss grows fat on a rollin' stone
   But that's not how it used to be
   When the jester sang for the king and queen
   In a coat he borrowed from James Dean
   And a voice that came from you and me
   Oh and while the king was looking down,
   The jester stole his thorny crown
   The courtroom was adjourned,
   No verdict was returned
   And while Lenin read a book on Marx
   The quartet practiced in the park
   And we sang dirges in the dark
   The day the music died
   We were singin'...bye-bye...etc.

3. Helter-skelter in the summer swelter
   The birds flew off with a fallout shelter
   Eight miles high and fallin' fast,
   It landed foul on the grass
   The players tried for a forward pass,
   With the jester on the sidelines in a cast
   Now the half-time air was sweet perfume
   While the sergeants played a marching tune
   We all got up to dance
   But we never got the chance
   'Cause the players tried to take the field,
   The marching band refused to yield
   Do you recall what was revealed
   The day the music died
   We started singin'... bye-bye...etc.

4. And there we were all in one place,
   A generation lost in space
   With no time left to start again
   So come on, Jack be nimble, Jack be quick,
   Jack Flash sat on a candlestick
   'Cause fire is the devil's only friend
   And as I watched him on the stage
   My hands were clenched in fits of rage
   No angel born in hell
   Could break that Satan's spell
   And as the flames climbed high into the night
   To light the sacrificial rite
   I saw Satan laughing with delight
   The day the music died
   He was singin'...bye-bye...etc.

Barely Breathing

Words and Music by
Duncan Sheik

Better Together

Words and Music by
Jack Johnson

se - pi - a - tone lov - ing. Love is the an - swer at least for most of the ques - tions in my heart, like,

"Why are we here?" and "Where do we go?" and "How come it's so hard?" And

it's not al - ways eas - y and some - times life can be de - ceiv - ing.

I'll tell you one thing: it's al - ways bet - ter when we're to - geth - er.

Mm, ___ it's al - ways bet - ter when we're to - geth - er.
Yeah, ___ it's al - ways bet - ter when we're to - geth - er.

Yeah, ___ we look at the stars when we're to - geth - er.)
Mm, ___ we're some - where in be - tween to - geth - er.)

Well, ___ it's al - ways bet - ter when we're to - geth - er.

Yeah, ___ it's al - ways bet - ter when we're to - geth - er. ___

know that they'll be gone ___ when the morn-ing light ___ sings ___ or brings new ___

___ things. ___ For to - mor - row night ___ you see ___ that

they'll be gone ___ too; ___ too man - y things I have to do. But if all of these

dreams ___ might find their way in - to my day - to - day scene, ___ I'd be

I could say, ___ but I will still tell you one thing: ___ We're bet - ter to - geth - er. ___

Black Water

Words and Music by
Patrick Simmons

Well, if it rains, I don't care, ___ don't make no

Blaze of Glory

featured in the film YOUNG GUNS II

Words and Music by
Jon Bon Jovi

wake up in the morn - ing and I raise my wea-ry head, ____ I've got an
night I go to bed, I pray the Lord my soul to keep. _ No, I ain't

catch me if ___ you can. I'm go - ing
seen it die ___ in vain. Shot

down in a blaze of glo -

\- ry. Take me now but know the truth. __

__ I'm go - ing out
'Cause I'm go - ing down
I'm go - ing out

in a blaze of

glo - ry. Lord, I nev - er drew first but I drew first blood,
and I'm
I'm the
and I'm

no one's son. Call me young gun.

dev-il's son. Call me young gun.

You

gun.

Guitar solo ad lib.

Play 3 times

Solo ends

N.C.

42

The Boxer

Words and Music by
Paul Simon

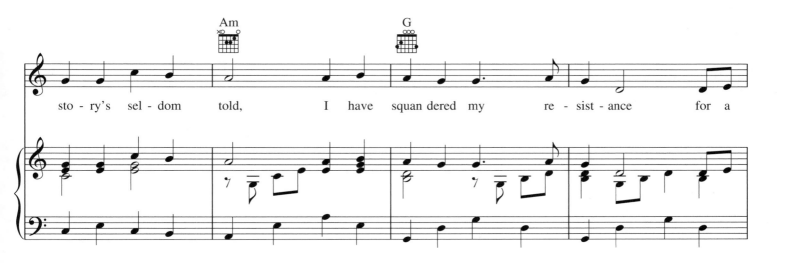

All lies and jest, still a man hears what he wants to hear, And dis - re - gards the rest. _____

When I left my home and my fam - i - ly, _____ I was

no more than a boy in the com - pa - ny ___ of stran - gers in the

qui - et of a rail - way sta - tion run - ning scared, _____

Lay - ing low, seek - ing out the poor - er quar - ters where the

rag - ged peo - ple go, Look - ing for the plac - es on - ly they would

47

go - ing home.

In the clear - ing stands a box - er, and a fight - er by his trade, And he car - ries the re - mind - ers of ev - 'ry glove that laid him down __ Or cut him till he cried __ out in his an - ger and his shame, __

Repeat and Fade

52

Brown Eyed Girl

Words and Music by
Van Morrison

Moderately

1. Hey where did we ___ go? Days ___ when the rains ___ came,

2., 3. (*See additional lyrics*)

down ___ in the hol-low play-in' a new ___ game,

laugh-ing and a - run-ning hey, ___ hey, skip-ping and a - jump-ing.

In the mist - y morn - ing fog __ with our hearts a-thump - in', and
you, my brown eyed girl. _____
You, my brown eyed girl. ___ Do you re mem -
- ber when we used to sing: ___ sha la ___ la la ___

Chorus

Additional Lyrics

2. Whatever happened to Tuesday and so slow
   Going down the old mine with a transistor radio
   Standing in the sunlight laughing
   Hiding behind a rainbow's wall
   Slipping and a-sliding
   All along the waterfall
   With you, my brown eyed girl
   You, my brown eyed girl.
   Do you remember when we used to sing:
   Chorus

3. So hard to find my way, now that I'm all on my own
   I saw you just the other day, my, how you have grown
   Cast my memory back there, Lord
   Sometime I'm overcome thinking 'bout
   Making love in the green grass
   Behind the stadium
   With you, my brown eyed girl
   With you, my brown eyed girl.
   Do you remember when we used to sing:
   Chorus

Burn One Down

Words and Music by
Ben Harper

Let us ___ burn one from end to end, and pass it o-ver to me, ___

*Guitarists: Tune down one whole step (low to high): D-G-C-F-A-D.

My choice __ is what I choose to do. And if it's caus-in' no harm, __ it should-n't
Herb, the __ gift from the earth, and what's from the earth __ is of the

both - er you. __ Your choice __ is who you choose to be. And if you're
great - est worth. __ So be - fore you __ knock it, try it first. Oh, you'll

To Coda

I'm gon-na burn ____ one… ____ Oh.

Repeat and fade

California Dreamin'

Words and Music by
John Phillips and Michelle Phillips

Cat's in the Cradle

Words and Music by
Harry Chapin and Sandy Chapin

He learned to walk while I   was a - way.   And he was   talk - in' 'fore I knew it.   And
lot   to   do."   He said,   "That's o - kay."   And he   walked a - way, but   his

as   he grew   he'd say,   "I'm   gon - na   be   like   you,   Dad.   You
smile nev - er dimmed. It said,   "I'm   gon - na   be   like   him,   yeah.   You

know I'm gon - na   be   like   you."   }
know I'm gon - na   be   like   him."   }
                                                    And the

cat's   in   the cra - dle   and the   sil - ver spoon,———   lit - tle boy   blue and the man———

68

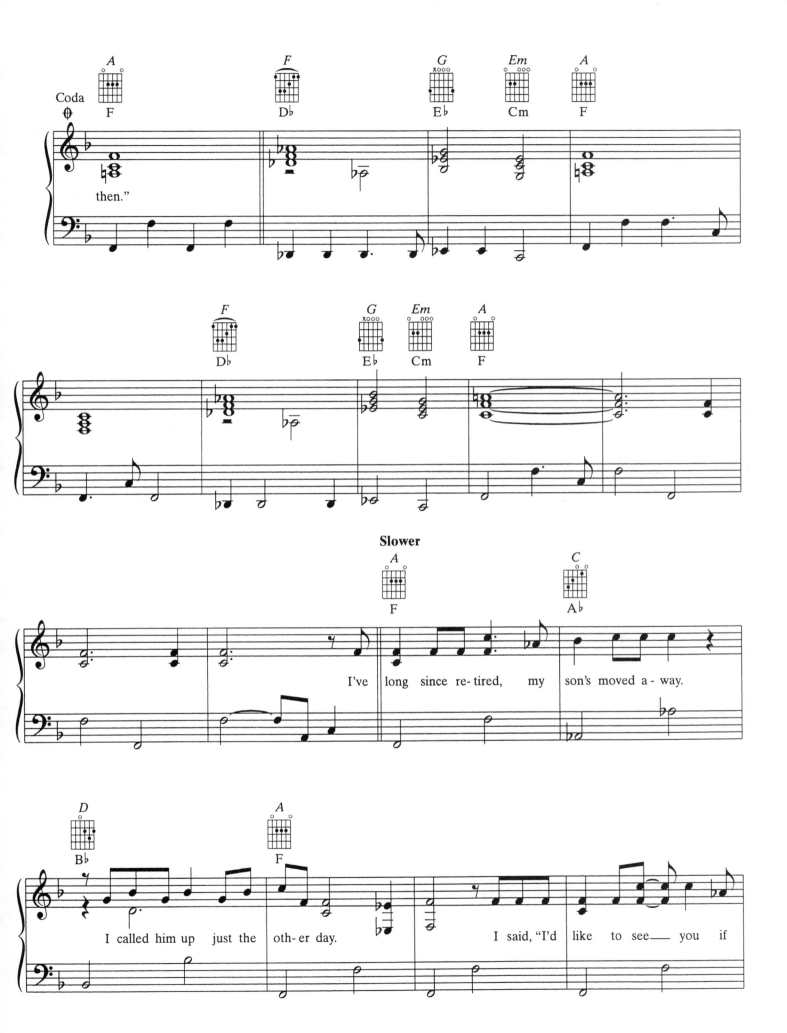

you don't mind." — He said, "I'd love to, Dad, — if I can find the time. —

You see, my new job's a has-sle and the kids have the flu, — but it's

sure nice talk-in' to you, Dad. It's been sure nice talk-in' to

you." And as I hung up the phone it oc-

Change the World

Words and Music by
Wayne Kirkpatrick, Gordon Kennedy
and Tommy Sims

But ____ for now I find _____
'Til then I'd be a fool _____

A/E   G#7

's on - ly in my ____ dreams ____
wish - ing for the ____ day ____

that I can

F#m7   G#7   C#m7

change _____ the world. ____

D#m7♭5   G#7   C#m

I { will / would / would } be ____ the sun - light in your u - ni - verse. _

ba - by, __ if I __ could __ change __

the __ world. __ *Guitar solo*

Solo ends I could

D.S. al Coda

Crash into Me

Words and Music by
David J. Matthews

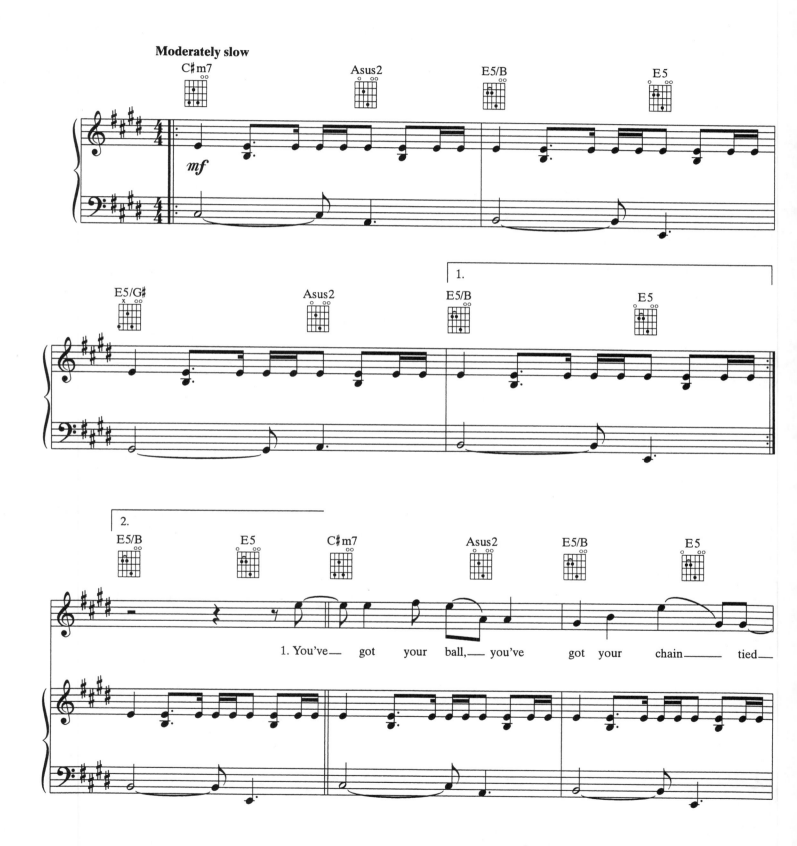

1. You've — got your ball, — you've got your chain — tied —

80

2. Touch your lips just so I know.
3. *See additional lyrics*

In your eyes, love, it glows so. I'm

bare-boned and cra-zy for

you.

Oh, when you come

Additional Lyrics

3. Only if I've gone overboard,
Then I'm begging you
To forgive me, oh,
In my haste.
When I'm holding you so, girl,
Close to me.
Oh, and you come... *(To Chorus)*

Crazy Little Thing Called Love

Words and Music by
Freddie Mercury

Moderately fast Shuffle

Oh, this thing _____ called called

love, well, I just _____ can't han - dle it. _____ This thing _____
love, it cries _____ in a cra - dle all night. It swings, _____

_____ called love, I _____ must _____ get a -
it jives, it shakes _____ all o - ver like a

round to it.___ I ain't___ read-y.
jel - ly - fish.___ I kind-a like it.

Cra - zy lit - tle thing called

love.

Well, this thing ___

There goes my ba - by; ___

she knows ___ how to rock and roll.___ She drives ___ me

cra - zy.___

She gives me hot and cold fe - ver. She

mo - tor bike __ un - til I'm read - y.   Cra - zy lit - tle thing called

love.

I got - ta be cool, ____ re - lax, ____ a - get hip, ____ a - get on my tracks. Take a back seat, ____ hitch - hike ____ to take a lit - tle long_ ride_ on my

motor bike ___ un-til I'm read - y.   Cra - zy lit - tle thing called

love.   This thing ____   called

love,   I ____ just _____ can't ___ han - dle it. ____ This

thing   called love,   I ____ must ____   get a -

94

round to it.___ I ain't___ read - y. Cra - zy lit - tle thing called

love, cra - zy lit - tle thing called love, cra -

- zy lit - tle thing called love, cra - zy lit - tle thing called

love, hey, cra - zy lit - tle thing called love.

Creep

Words and Music by
Scott Weiland, Dean DeLeo,
Robert DeLeo and Eric Kretz

Slow Rock Ballad

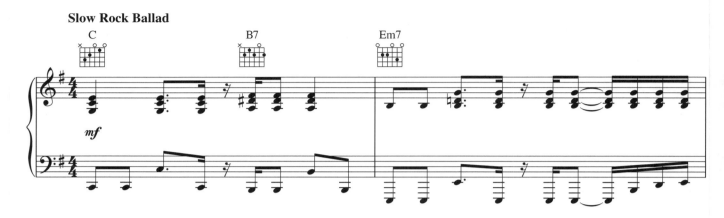

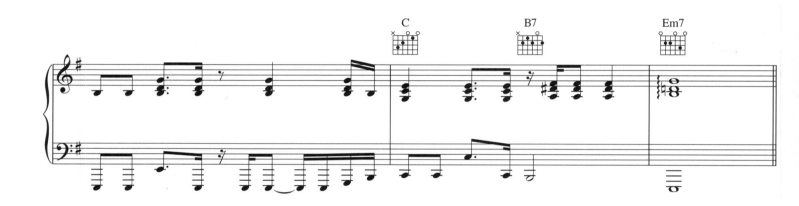

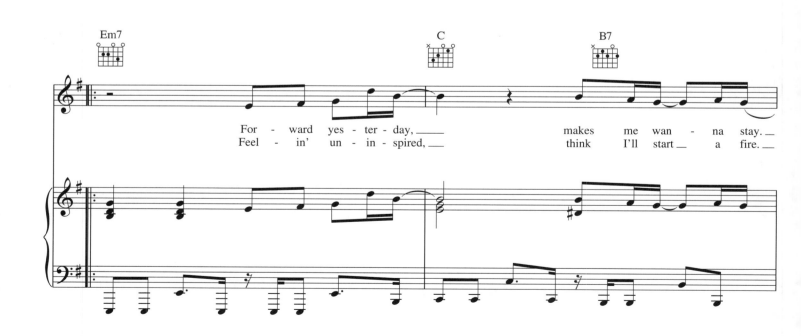

For - ward yes - ter - day, _____ makes me wan - na stay. _____
Feel - in' un - in - spired, _____ think I'll start _ a fire. _____

Dance with Me

Words and Music by
John and Johanna Hall

101

1, 2, 4

dance with _ me. _____   *Instrumental ends*

3, 5

dance with _ me. _____   *Instrumental ends*

Let it ____ lift _____ you _____ off the ___ ground. _

Star - ry ___ eyes, ___ and love is all ___ a - round ___ us.

102

Daughter

Words and Music by Stone Gossard,
Jeffrey Ament, Eddie Vedder,
Michael McCready and David Abbruzzese

Dust in the Wind

Words and Music by
Kerry Livgren

Moderate Folk style

111

Ev - 'ry - thing _ is dust in the wind.
wind.)

Repeat and Fade

Optional Ending

poco rit.

Free Fallin'

Words and Music by
Tom Petty and Jeff Lynne

It's a long day ___
vam - pires ___
glide down ___

liv - in' in Re - se - da. There's a free - way ___ run - nin' through the yard. ___ And I'm a
walk - in' through the val - ley move ___ west down ___ Ven - tur - a Boul - e - vard. And all the
o - ver Mul - hol - land. I wan - na write her ___ name in the sky. ___ I wan - na

bad boy ___ 'cause I don't e - ven miss ___ her. I'm a bad boy ___ for
bad boys ___ are stand - ing in the shad - ows. And the good girls ___ are
free fall ___ out in - to noth - in'. Gon - na leave this ___

Homeward Bound

Words and Music by
Paul Simon

I'm sit - tin' in the rail - way sta - tion, got a tick - et for my
Ev - 'ry day's an end - less stream __ of cig - a - rettes and
night I'll sing my songs a - gain, __ I'll play the game

des - ti - na - tion. ____ Mm. _____
mag - a - zines. _____ Mm. _____
and pre - tend. _____ Mm. _____

On a tour __ of one - night stands my suit - case and gui - tar __
And each town looks __ the same to me; the mov - ies and the fac -
But all my words __ come back to me in shades of me - di - oc -

es - cap - ing, home where my mu - sic's play - ing, home where my love

lies wait - ing si - lent - ly for me. (3.) To

Si - lent - ly for me.

I'm Yours

Words and Music by
Jason Mraz

Moderately slow, with a Reggae feel

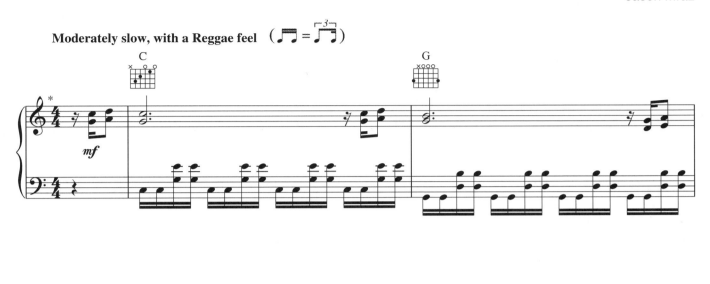

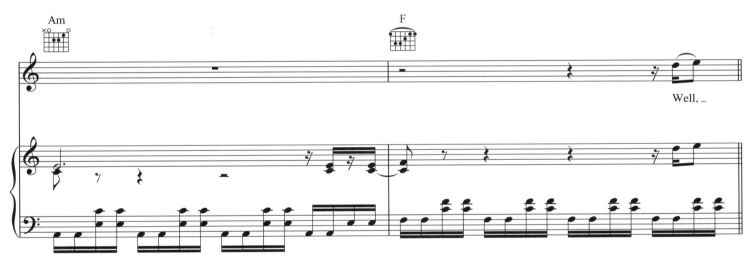

Well,

you done done me in; you bet I felt it. I tried to be chill, but you're so hot that I melt-ed. I

*Recorded a half step lower.

more. _ It can - not wait. I'm yours. _____

Well, o - pen up your mind and see _ like me. ____ O - pen up your plans and, damn, _ you're free.

dear, and I will nib - ble your ear. _____ *Scat sing...*

I've been spend - ing

way too long __ check - ing my tongue in the mir - ror and bend - ing o - ver back - wards just to try to see it clear - er. But

my breath fogged up the glass, and so I drew a new face and I laughed. I

guess what I'll be say-ing is there ain't no bet-ter rea-son to rid your-self of van-i-ties and just go with the sea-sons. It's

what we aim to do. Our name is our vir-tue. But

I won't hes-i-tate no more, no

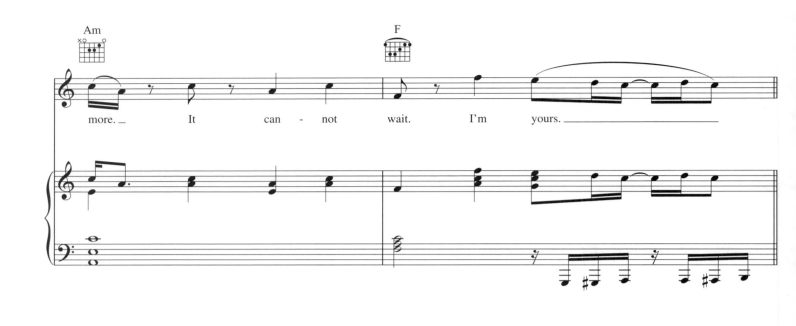

more. _ It can - not wait. I'm yours. _____

O - pen up your mind and see like me. _ O - pen up your plans and, damn, _ you're _ free. _
(I won't hes - i - tate no more, no

___ Look in - to your heart _ and you'll _ find _ that the sky _ is yours. _____ So
more. It can - not wait. I'm sure. _____ No

I Walk the Line

Words and Music by
John R. Cash

Additional Lyrics

3. As sure as night is dark and day is light,
   I keep you on my mind both day and night.
   And happiness I've known proves that it's right.
   Because you're mine I walk the line.

4. You've got a way to keep me on your side.
   You give me cause for love that I can't hide.
   For you I know I'd even try to turn the tide.
   Because you're mine I walk the line.

5. I keep a close watch on this heart of mine.
   I keep my eyes wide open all the time.
   I keep the ends out for the tie that binds.
   Because you're mine I walk the line.

I've Just Seen a Face

Words and Music by
John Lennon and Paul McCartney

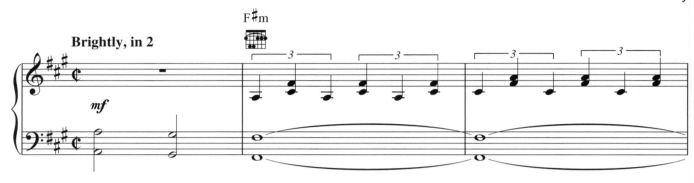

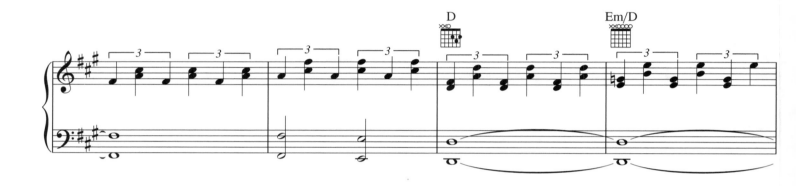

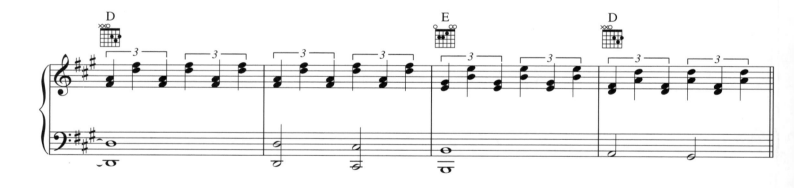

I've just seen a face, I can't for-get the time ___ or

Iris
from the Motion Picture CITY OF ANGELS

Words and Music by
John Rzeznik

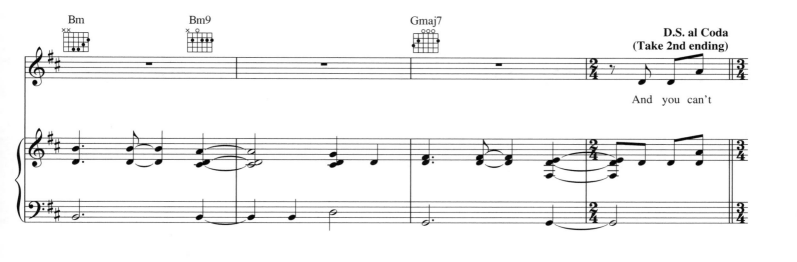

And you can't

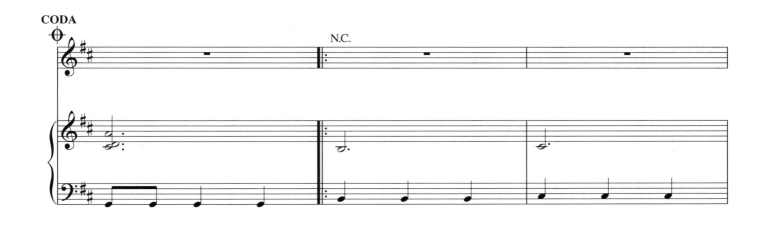

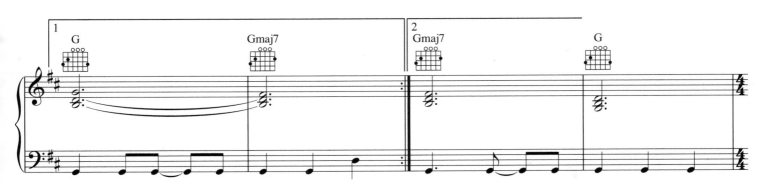

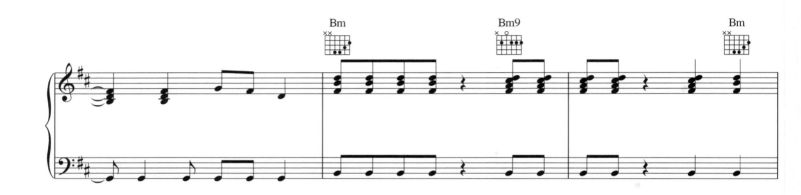

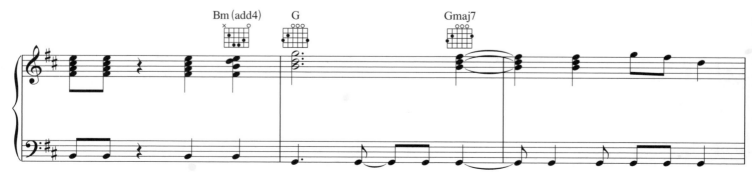

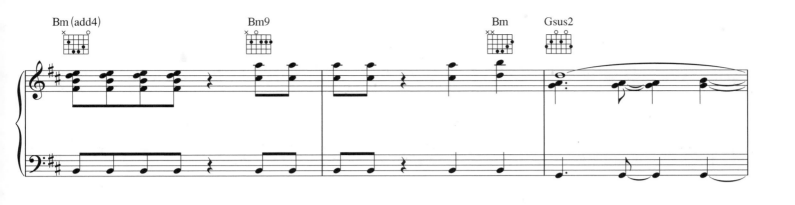

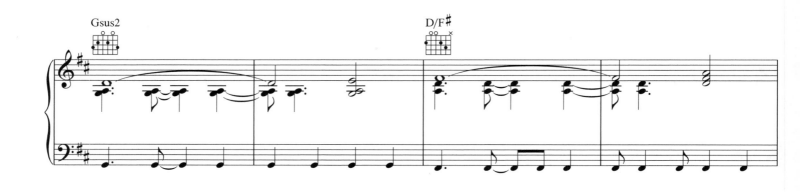

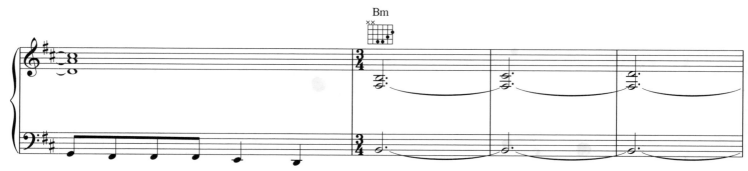

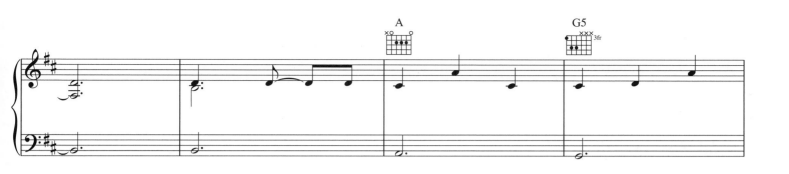

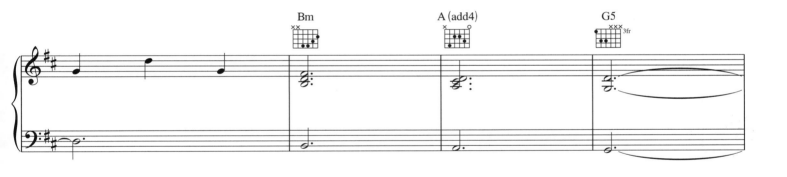

And I _____ don't want the world _____ to see _____ me

'cause I _____ don't _____ think that they'd _____ un - der - stand.

When ev - 'ry - thing's _____ made to be _____ bro - ken

I just _____ want _____ you to know _____ who I _____

am. _____ And I _____

146

Jack and Diane

Words and Music by
John Mellencamp

A lit - tle dit - ty a - bout Jack and Di - ane, ___ two A - mer - i - can kids grow - in' up

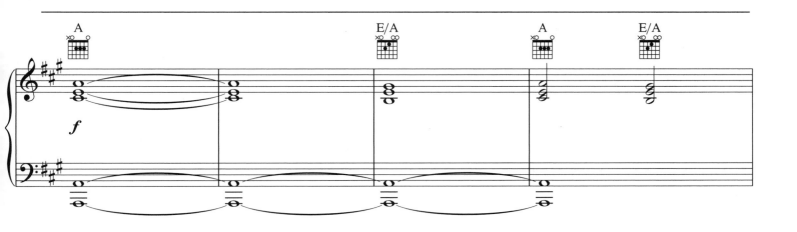

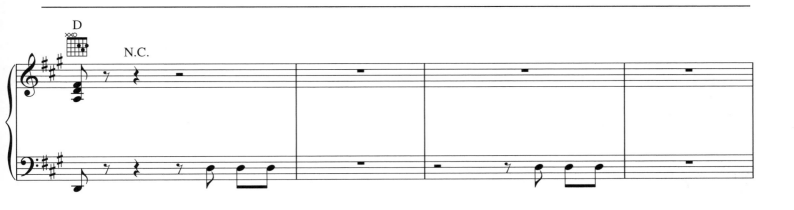

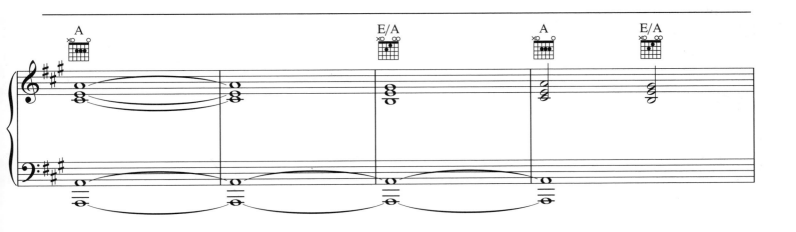

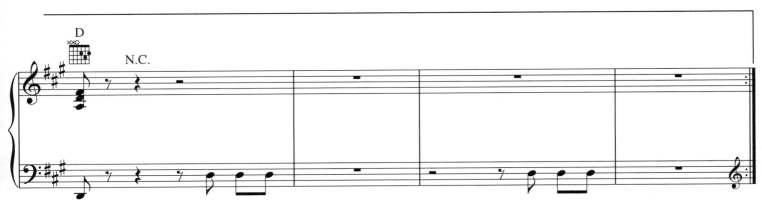

change is com - in' 'round real soon, make us wom - en and men.

D.S. al Coda

CODA

A lit - tle

ditty a-bout Jack and Di - ane, _____

two A-mer-i-can kids do-in' the best that they _ can.

Repeat and Fade

N.C.

156

Landslide

Words and Music by
Stevie Nicks

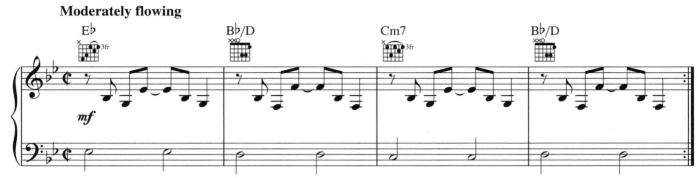

I took my love ____ and I took it down. ____

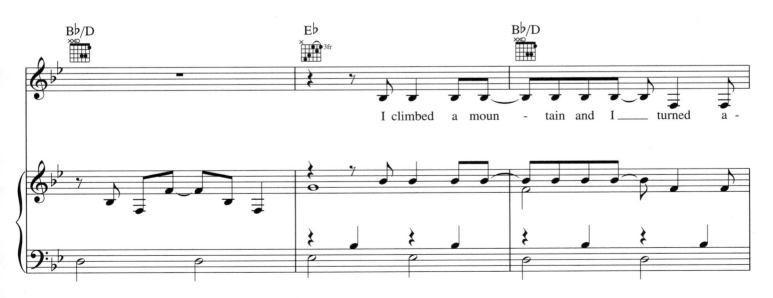

I climbed a moun - tain and I ____ turned a -

round. ___ And I saw my ___ re - flec -

- tion in the snow - cov - ered hills ___ till the

land - slide brought me down. ___

Oh, mir - ror in ___ the sky, ___ what is

if you see ___ my re- flec - tion in the snow - cov - ered hills, ___ well, the land - slide will bring it down, ___ down. ___ And if you see ___ my re- flec - tion in the snow -

rall.

164

Me and Bobby McGee

Words and Music by
Kris Kristofferson and Fred Foster

Busted flat in Baton Rouge, waitin' for a train, when I's feelin' near as faded as my jeans. Bobby thumbed a diesel down just before it rained. It rode us all the way into New Orleans. I

* Vocal written one octave higher than sung.

168

Lord.

More Than a Feeling

Words and Music by
Tom Scholz

lost my-self____ in a fa - mil - iar song.
I still re-call____ as I wan-der on,

closed my__ eyes___ and I slipped a - way.____
clear as the sun__ in the sum-mer__ sky.____

It's more than a feel - ing_____ when I
(More than a feel - ing.)_____

hear that old song_____ they used to play,_____ and
(More than a feel - ing.)_____

I be - gin dream - ing_____ till I
(More than a feel - ing.)_____

see Mar - i - anne_____ walk_____ a - way. I see my Mar-

When I'm tired—— and think - ing cold, I hide in my mu - sic, for-

More Than Words

Words and Music by
Nuno Bettencourt and Gary Cherone

Lyrics:

Say - in' "I ____ love _____ you" is
Now that I've __ tried _____ to

not the words _ I want __ to __ hear __ from you. ____ It's not that I ____
talk to you __ and make __ you __ un - der - stand, ____ all __ you __

Recorded a half step lower.

Only the Good Die Young

Words and Music by
Billy Joel

Come out Vir-gin-ia don't let me wait ___ You Cath-o-lic girls ___ start
showed you a stat-ue told you to pray ___ They built you a tem-ple and

good die young _ You got a nice white dress and a
good die young _ *(Instrumental)*

par - ty on your con - fir - ma - tion _____ You've got a

brand new soul _____ and a cross of gold _____

_____ *(End instrumental)*
But Vir - gin - ia they did - n't give you quite e - nough in - for - ma -
Said your moth - er told you all that I could give you was a rep - u - ta -

195

Patience

Words and Music by
W. Axl Rose, Slash, Izzy Stradlin',
Duff McKagan and Steven Adler

Said, sug - ar,___ make it slow___ and we come to - geth - er fine.

All we need___ is just___ a lit - tle pa -

tience.

1.

Moderately slow, in 4

Repeat and fade

* *Vocal ad lib (see additional lyrics)*

*Enter 3rd time

Additional Lyrics

2. I sit here on the stairs 'cause I'd rather be alone.
   If I can't have you right now I'll wait, dear.
   Sometimes I get so tense but I can't speed up the time.
   But you know, love, there's one more thing to consider.

   Said, woman, take it slow and things will be just fine.
   You and I'll just use a little patience.
   Said, sugar, take the time 'cause the lights are shining bright.
   You and I've got what it takes to make it.
   We won't fake it, ah, I'll never break it 'cause I can't take it.

Vocal ad lib:

Little patience, mm, yeah, mm, yeah.
Need a little patience, yeah.
Just a little patience, yeah.
Some more patience.
I been walkin' the streets at night
Just tryin' to get it right.
Hard to see with so many around.
You know I don't like being stuck in the ground,
And the streets don't change, but baby the name.
I ain't got time for the game 'cause I need you.
Yeah, yeah, but I need you, oo, I need you.
Woh, I need you, oo, this time.

Pinball Wizard

Words and Music by
Peter Townshend

Question

Words and Music by
Justin Hayward

Why do we ne - ver get an an - swer when we're knock-ing at the door? There's a thou - sand mil - lion ques - tions a - bout hate and death and war. 'Cause when we

stop and look a - round us there is no - thing that we need In a world of per - se - cu - tion that is burn - ing in its greed.

Ah,

Ah,

Ah ——————— ah —— ah ——

Why do we ne - ver get —— an an - swer —— when we're

knock - ing at _____ the door? _____ Be-cause the truth is hard _____ to swal-

- low. _____ That's what the war of love _____ is for! _____

It's not the

way _____ that you say _____ it when you do those things to me, It's more the way _____ that you mean _____ it when you
si - lence of the moun-tains and the crash-ing of the sea There lies a land I once lived _____ in and she's

tell me what will be. And when you stop and think a-bout_ it you won't be-lieve it's true That all the
wait-ing there for me. But in the grey___ of the morn-ing my mind be-comes con-fused Be-tween the

love you've been giv-ing___ has all been meant for you. I'm look-ing for some-one to change my
dead and the sleep-ing and the road that I must choose.

p cresc. poco a poco ------

life, I'm look-ing for a mir-a-cle in my life And if you_ could

see what it's done to me To lose the love I knew you'd safe-ly lead me

poco rall.-----

f

Reason to Believe

Words and Music by
Tim Hardin

that you ___ lied straight - faced while I cried. ___

Still I look to find a rea -

son to be - lieve. Some - one like

you makes it hard to live with - out

2. *Violin solo*

some-bod-y else. Some-one like   you   makes it

eas-y to give, __   nev-er think   a-bout my - self. __

D(add9)   G   D

If I   gave __ you   time __ to change my mind, __
Solo ends If I   lis-tened   long e-nough __ to   you, __

G   C

__ I'd   find a way __   just   to leave __
__ I'd   find a way __   to   be - lieve __

the past be - hind.
that it's all true.

Know-ing that you lied straight -

faced while I cried. Still I

look to find a rea-son to be - lieve.

214

215

Redemption Song

Words and Music by
Bob Marley

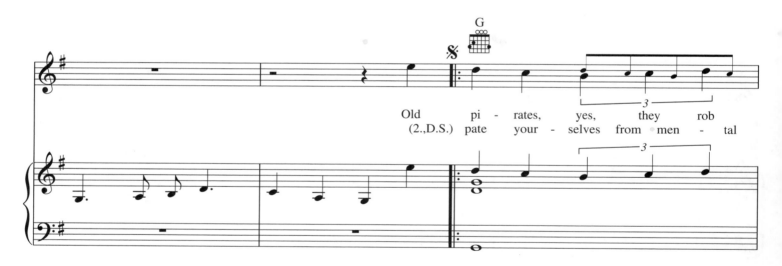

Old pi - rates, yes, they rob
(2.,D.S.) pate your - selves from men - tal

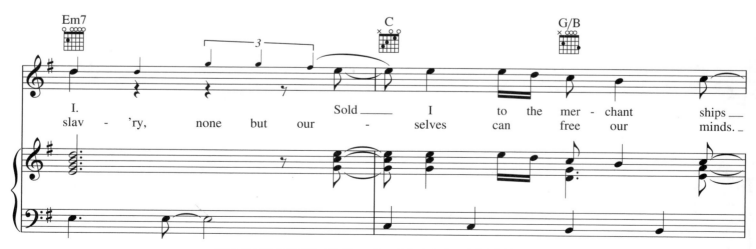

1.
slav - 'ry, none but our - Sold   I   to the mer - chant   selves can free our   ships   minds.

Return of the Grievous Angel

Words and Music by
Gram Parsons and Thomas S. Brown

225

man waved his lan-tern good-bye ____ and good day ____ as we went roll - ing through. ____

Bill - boards and truck - stops pass ____ by the griev - ous an - gel,

and now I know ____ just what I have ____ to do.

D.S. al Coda I

And the

226

227

Still the Same

Words and Music by
Bob Seger

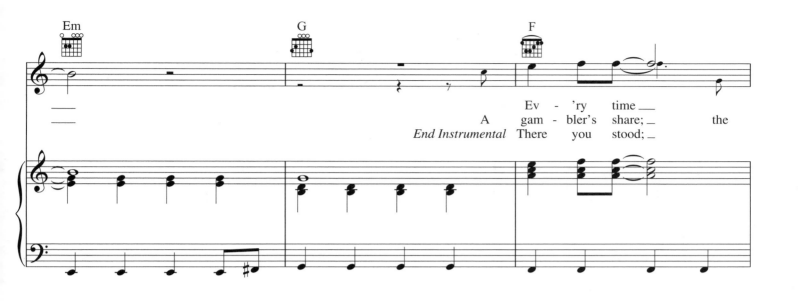

Em / G / F

Ev - 'ry time ___
A gam - bler's share; ___ the
End Instrumental There you stood; ___

G / C / E

they were sure they had you caught, ___
on - ly risk that you would take, ___
ev - 'ry - bod - y watched you play. ___

you were quick - er than they thought. ___
the on - ly loss you could for - sake, ___
I just turned and walked a - way. ___

Am / Dm / G / **To Coda** $\oplus$

the
You'd just turn your back and walk. ___
the on - ly bluff you could - n't fake. ___
I had noth - ing left to say. ___

231

Summer Breeze

Words and Music by
James Seals and Dash Crofts

See the cur - tains hang - in' in the win - dow ____ in the eve - ning on a Fri - day night. ____
See the pa - per lay - in' on the side - walk, ____ a lit - tle mu - sic from the house next door. ____

A lit - tle light a shin - in' through the win - dow
So I walk on up to the door - step, ____

makes me feel fine, _____ blow - in' through the jas - mine in my

mind. _____

Sweet days of sum - mer the jas - mine's in bloom, ___

food cook-in' and the plates for two.

Feel the arms that reach ___ out to hold ___ me ___ in the eve-ning when the day is through. ___

Sum-mer breeze ___

makes me feel fine, ___ blow-in' through the jas-mine in my

Sunshine

(Go Away Today)

Written by
Jonathan Edwards

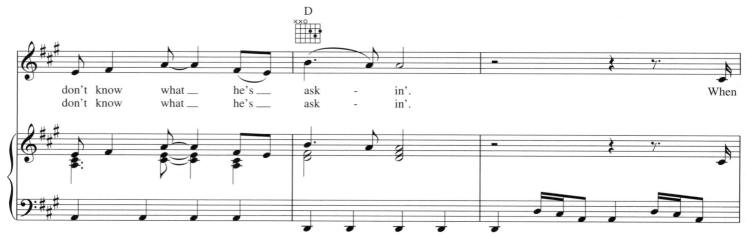

he tells me ____ I bet - ter get in line, ____ I can't hear what ____ he's ____
Work - in' starts ____ to make me won - der where ____ the fruits of what I do are
Sun - shine, come ____ on back an - oth - er day, ____ I prom - ise you ____ I'll be ____

say - in'. When I grow up, ____ I'm gon - na make it mine, ____ or
go - in'. He says in love ____ and war ____ all is fair, ____ but
sing - in'. This old world, _ she's gon - na turn a - round; _

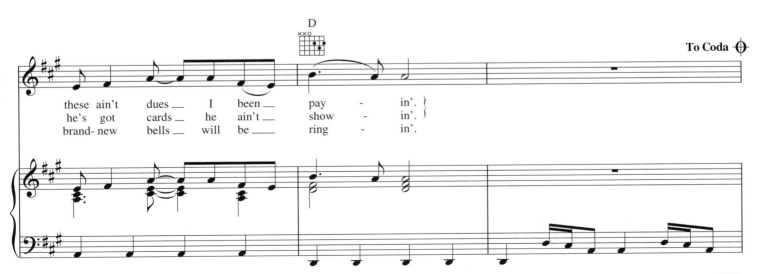

To Coda

these ain't dues ____ I been ____ pay - in'. }
he's got cards ____ he ain't ____ show - in'. }
brand- new bells ____ will be ____ ring - in'.

How much does it ___ cost? ___ I'll buy ___ it. The time is all ___ we've ___ lost. ___

___ I'll try ___ it, 'n' he can't e - ven run ___ his own ___ life; ___ I'll be

damned if he'll ___ run mine! ___   Sun - shine, ___   Sun - shine, ___

D.S. al Coda

CODA

Take Me Home, Country Roads

Words and Music by
John Denver, Bill Danoff
and Taffy Nivert

Teach Your Children

Words and Music by
Graham Nash

You

who are on the road

must have a code ____ that ____ you can live by, and so be - come ____ your - self, be - cause ____ the past ____ is just a good - bye.

250

Time in a Bottle

Words and Music by
Jim Croce

find them. _____ I've

looked a - round e - nough to know that you're the one I want to go through

time with. If

I had a box just for wish - es _____ and

The Times They Are A-Changin'

Words and Music by
Bob Dylan

1. Come gath-er 'round peo-ple where-
2.-5. (See additional lyrics)

ev-er you roam _____ and ad-mit that the

wa-ters a-round you have grown. And ac-cept it that

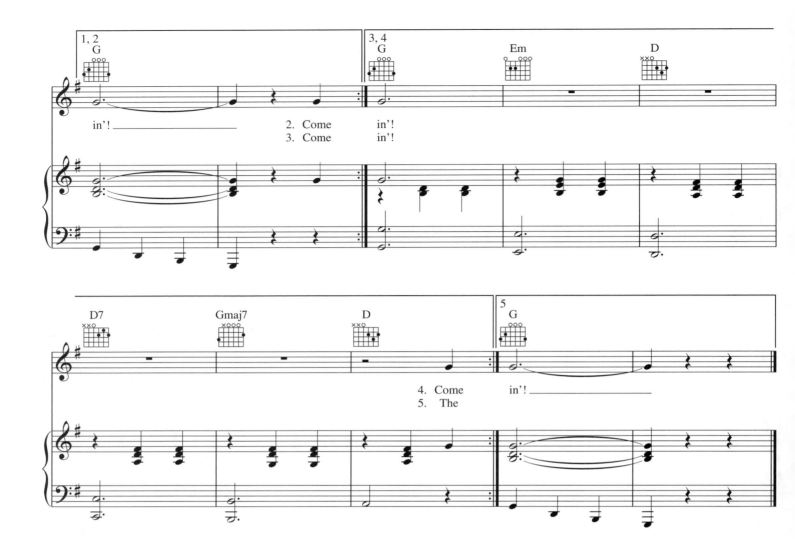

Additional Lyrics

2. Come writers and critics
   Who prophesy with your pen
   And keep your eyes wide
   The chance won't come again.
   And don't speak too soon
   For the wheel's still in spin,
   And there's no tellin' who
   That it's namin'.
   For the loser now
   Will be later to win
   For the times they are a-changin'.

3. Come senators, congressmen
   Please heed the call
   Don't stand in the doorway
   Don't block up the hall.
   For he that gets hurt
   Will be he who has stalled,
   There's a battle
   Outside and it's ragin'.
   It'll soon shake your windows
   And rattle your walls
   For the times they are a-changin'!

4. Come mothers and fathers,
   Throughout the land
   And don't criticize
   What you can't understand.
   Your sons and your daughters
   Are beyond your command,
   Your old road is
   Rapidly agin'.
   Please get out of the new one
   If you can't lend your hand
   For the times they are a-changin'!

5. The line it is drawn
   The curse it is cast
   The slow one now will
   Later be fast.
   As the present now
   Will later be past,
   The order is rapidly fadin'.
   And the first one now
   Will later be last
   For the times they are a-changin'!

To Be with You

Words and Music by
Eric Martin and David Grahame

be with you. _____ Deep in - side I hope you'll

feel ___ it, too. ___ Wait - ed on a line ___ of

greens and blues _____ just to be the next to be ___ with you, ___

just to be the next to ___ be with you. ___ Ooh.

rall.

Toes

Words and Music by
Zac Brown, Wyatt Durrette,
John Driskell Hopkins and Shawn Mullins

*Recorded a half step lower.

265

in the sand. Not a wor-ry in the world, a cold beer in my hand. Life is good

to-day. Life is good to-day.

Ad-i-os and va-ya con Di-os.

Yeah, I'm leav-ing G - A.
A long way from G - A.
Go-ing home now to stay.

And if it weren't for te-qui-la and
Yes, and all the mu-cha-chas, they
The se-ño-ri-tas don't *quie-ro* when

pret-ty se-ño-ri-tas, ___ I'd, I'd have no rea-son __ to stay. _____
call me __ "Big Pop-pa" ___ when I throw pe-sos __ their way. ___
there's no __ *di-ne-ro,* ___ yeah, and I got no mon-ey to stay. ___

Tacet

Ad-i-os and va-ya ___ con Di-os.

Yeah, I'm leav-ing G-A. ___
A long way __ from G-A. ___
Go-ing home _ now to stay. _

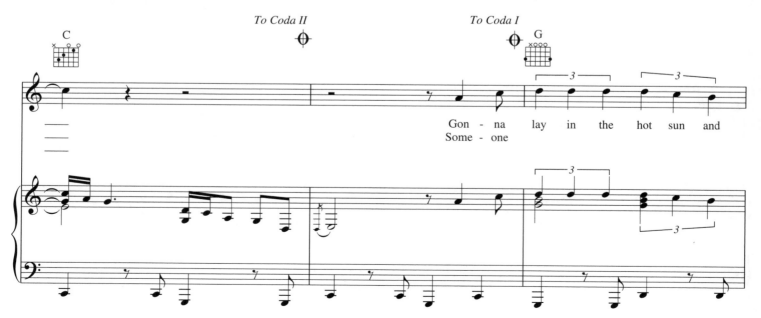

To Coda II   *To Coda I*

Gon-na lay in the hot sun and
Some-one

271

Coda II

(Spoken:) Just gonna drive up by the lake and put my

ass in a lawn chair, toes in the clay. Not a wor - ry in the world, a P - B -

R on the way. Life is good to - day. Life is good to - day.

The Way I Am

Words and Music by
Ingrid Michaelson

love ____ the way ____ you say ____ good morn-ing, ____ and
____ love ____ the way.) ____

you ____ take me the way I am.

If you ____ are chill - y, ____

here, take my sweat-er. ____ Your head ____ is ach-

ing, _____ I'll make it bet - ter. _____ 'Cause

I _____ love _____ the way ____ you call ___ me "ba -
(I _____ love _____ the way.) ____

by," _____ and you _____ take me the way I

am.

We Can Work It Out

Words and Music by
John Lennon and Paul McCartney

You've Got a Friend

Words and Music by
Carole King

*Cues 2nd time only

282